Journeys Through
SPACE

McGraw Hill | **Wright Group**

The **McGraw-Hill** Companies

www.WrightGroup.com

 **Wright Group**

Copyright © 2011 by The McGraw-Hill Companies, Inc.

Printed in China.

Send all inquiries to:
Wright Group/McGraw-Hill
P.O. Box 812960
Chicago, IL 60681

ISBN 978-0-07-656408-8
MHID 0-07-656408-8

3 4 5 6 7 8 9 DSS 16 15 14 13 12 11

The *McGraw·Hill* Companies

Contents

Why do people study space?

Have you ever looked into the night sky and wondered about it? What are the stars made of? Where did they come from? Over the centuries, people have come up with many ideas about the night sky. Some of these ideas are being changed as scientists learn more.

Focus Questions

Selection ➊

What patterns and cycles do we find in space?

Selection ➋

How did people of the past explain objects in the night sky?

Selection ➌

How do people view space today?

Selection ➍

How might space be a part of our future?

 Preview ▶

 online coach

What patterns and cycles do we find in space? Preview pages 6–27. Then read *The Man Who Loved Astronomy* to find out.

THE MAN WHO LOVED
ASTRONOMY

BY JANA MARTIN

CHAPTER
1

What Is Astronomy?

Astronomy is the study of space. A person who studies space is called an **astronomer.** Astronomers study stars and planets. They also study moons and galaxies.

Mercury Venus Earth Mars Jupiter Saturn Uranus Neptune

Sun

Astronomers have found that Earth, Mars, Jupiter, Saturn, Uranus, and Neptune all have moons.

By 1930 astronomers knew of eight planets in our solar system. They knew that all eight planets **revolve,** or circle, around the sun. They knew that all eight planets **rotate,** or spin, as they move.

7

In the 1800s astronomers thought there might be a ninth planet. But no one could prove anything until 1930.

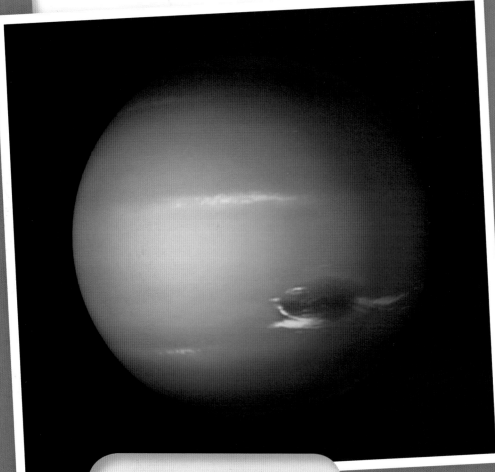

Strange occurrences in Neptune's path around the sun led scientists to believe another planet existed.

Who Is Clyde Tombaugh?

Clyde Tombaugh found what people thought was the ninth planet. He was just twenty-four years old at the time of his discovery.

Tombaugh grew up on a farm. He was **intrigued** by space from childhood. His father supported his interest in space. His uncle supported him too.

Clyde Tombaugh as a young man

Tombaugh learned about the stars and the planets. He watched them carefully. He borrowed his first **telescope** from his uncle. He spent hours looking through it. He was in **awe** of the sky.

Strategy Tool Kit
Make Connections
Do you find the sky interesting? Why or why not?

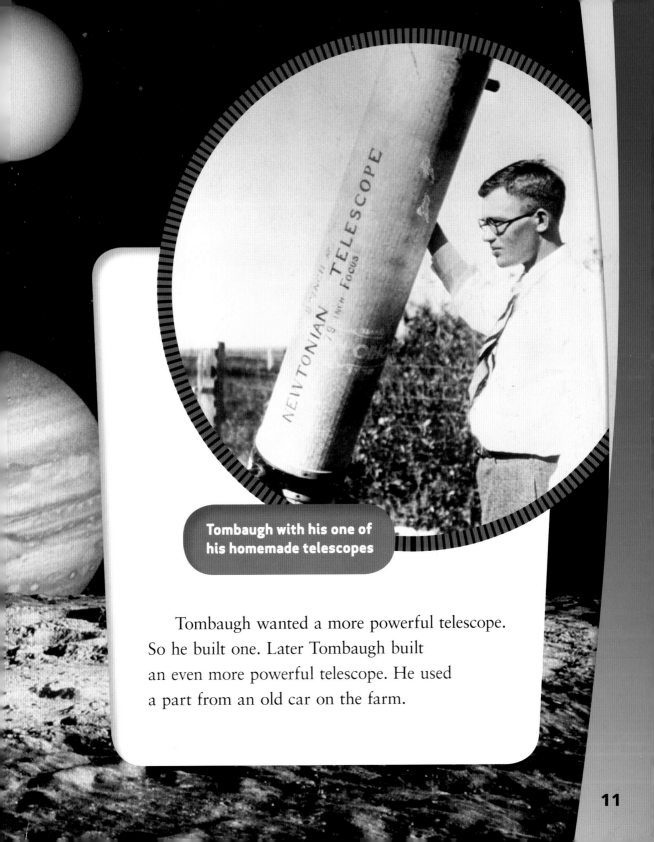

Tombaugh with his one of his homemade telescopes

Tombaugh wanted a more powerful telescope. So he built one. Later Tombaugh built an even more powerful telescope. He used a part from an old car on the farm.

Tombaugh's new telescope **improved** his view of Jupiter and Mars. He made many drawings of what he saw.

Tombaugh had not gone to college yet. He was **eager** to learn new ideas about space.

Mars

Jupiter

He sent his drawings to the Lowell Observatory in Arizona. An observatory is a place where astronomers study the sky. The astronomers at Lowell Observatory liked Tombaugh's drawings very much. They offered him a job.

The Anderson Mesa Station is part of the Lowell Observatory. The roof rolls back so telescopes can point to the sky.

3

Discovering Pluto

The telescopes at the Lowell Observatory were more **sophisticated** than any Tombaugh had ever seen. They were also bigger. The observatory also had hundreds of pictures of the night sky.

At the Lowell Observatory, visitors can still use a Clark telescope, the observatory's first telescope.

Many of the pictures were taken through telescopes. It became Tombaugh's job to take even more pictures.

People at the Lowell Observatory were interested in finding a possible ninth planet. They called it Planet X. Astronomers searched for it by recording patterns in the sky.

They needed two pictures for each small **section** in the sky. The pictures had to be taken a few days apart. Then they would be compared.

Usually the two pictures would look similar. The astronomers were looking for differences. They wanted to find one object that had moved. An object that moved could be a planet.

Tombaugh took the necessary pictures. He photographed the sky one tiny section at a time. It was hard work.

Tombaugh took pictures by using a camera in the telescope.

Stop and Think

How do you think Tombaugh's early interests helped him with this work?

Tombaugh worked with a large telescope. It was in the **dome** of the observatory. The dome was not heated. Sometimes it was very cold. He took many photographs.

This is the dome at the Lowell Observatory where Tombaugh worked.

A blink machine compares two photographs of the same area in space.

Then he used a blink machine to compare the patterns. The machine let him look from one picture to another very quickly.

Tombaugh spent about 7,000 hours looking at pictures. He did the same task over and over. It was often boring work.

task: job

One February day in 1930 Tombaugh compared two pictures. The patterns were different. One object was in a different place. He had found Planet X! News of the discovery traveled all over the world.

Planet X needed a name. Venetia Burney, a schoolgirl in England, suggested the name *Pluto*.

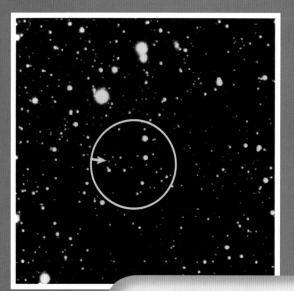 

These are the two photos that Tombaugh compared. The arrow in each photo points to Pluto.

Strategy Tool Kit
Monitor Comprehension
Explain the steps that Tombaugh followed to find Planet X. Reread pages 15–20 to check your understanding.

A LITTLE GIRL NAMES A PLANET

Venetia Burney suggested the name *Pluto* when she was just eleven years old. Pluto is the name of a Roman god.

Venetia's grandfather helped get her suggestion to the Lowell Observatory. The people there thought it was perfect. It matched the names of the rest of the planets, which were also named for Roman gods.

CHAPTER 4

A New Definition

Pluto was called our ninth planet
from 1930 to 2006. But then the definition,
or meaning, of the word *planet* changed.
Pluto did not fit into the new definition.

Mars is a planet.
It clears its path
as it circles the sun.

A planet is a round object
that circles a star, such as the sun.
A planet is large enough to clear its path
around the sun. It uses **gravity** to absorb
smaller objects into itself. This is how
it clears its path.

absorb: draw in

Pluto is a round object. It circles the sun.
But Pluto is not strong enough to clear its path.
Pluto is now thought of as a dwarf,
or small, planet.

Information written about Pluto before 2006 has had to be changed.

Strategy Tool Kit
Make Connections

In what ways is Pluto similar to other planets? In what ways is it different from other planets?

A dwarf planet has some gravity.
But it is not enough to clear its own path.
That means there are rocks in its path
that the dwarf planet is not able to absorb.

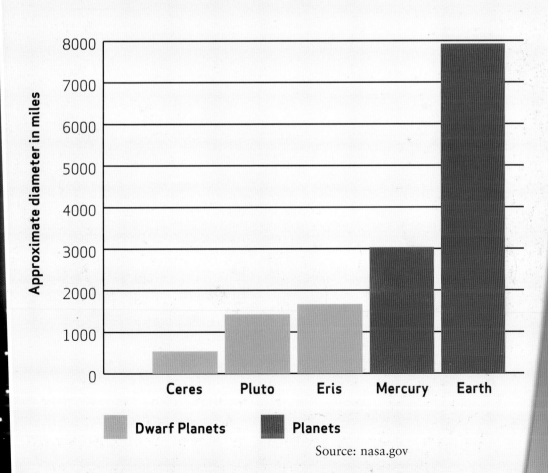

SIZES OF SOME PLANETS AND DWARF PLANETS

Approximate diameter in miles

Ceres Pluto Eris Mercury Earth

Dwarf Planets   Planets

Source: nasa.gov

Tombaugh's discovery of Pluto was exciting. He continued to study the patterns and cycles in space. He later discovered a cluster of galaxies. He also discovered 775 asteroids and a **comet**.

cluster: group

Some comets can be seen without a telescope.

Clyde Tombaugh, 1906–1997

Tombaugh died in 1997. He died before
it was decided that Pluto was a dwarf planet.
Some people thought the change
would have upset him. His family
did not think so. They said Tombaugh understood
that astronomy changes over time. That's
what made it so interesting to him.

Think Back
Selection 1

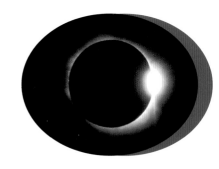

A Check Understanding ★

Make a list of the patterns and cycles Clyde Tombaugh found while studying space. PRACTICE COMPANION 293

B Understand Text Features ★★

Look at the bar graph on page 25. Show the bar graph to a partner. Explain what information in the text the graph helps you understand.

C Share and Compare ★★

Compare your list of patterns and cycles with a partner's list. Are any of the patterns and cycles the same? Are any different? Explain why.

D Think Critically ★★★★

Why do people study space? Use examples from the selection to explain.

My Home Page

Focus Question: How did people of the past explain objects in the night sky?

Selection Connection

You have learned about the kinds of discoveries scientists made about patterns and cycles in space. In the next selection you will learn why people study space.

Show What You Know

Think about the following: *the moon, the stars,* and *the sky at night.* Do you know any stories about these things? Write your ideas. PRACTICE COMPANION 294

Preview

How did people of the past explain objects in the night sky?
Preview pages 30–53. Then read *Looking at the Moon* to find out.

Looking at the
MOON

by Karen Baicker

CHAPTER 1

Thinking about the Moon

Look at the sky on a clear night. The first thing you <u>notice</u> may be the moon. The moon may be large and round. Or it may look thin and curved.

Why does the moon look different at different times? How old is the moon? What makes moonlight? People have asked questions about the moon for thousands of years.

notice: see

Sometimes the moon looks
like a narrow sliver.

Sometimes you can see the moon
in the daytime.

Today science has given us some
of the answers. But in the past people made up
stories to explain the mysteries of the sky.

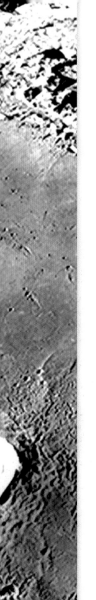

Faces in the Moon

The light and shadows on the moon create different shapes. Some people see a face when they look at the moon. Some **myths** tell about the moon. One Chinese myth tells about the moon goddess Chang'e.

Look at this picture of the moon. See if you can make out the face created by the light and shadows.

The yellow lines mark the shape of a rabbit created by the moon's surface.

Chang'e was **immortal**. Then she was sent to Earth. She lived as a human. She wanted to be immortal again. She took a pill that was given to her husband. She floated to the moon. She could not come back. She still lives there. Her friend rabbit lives there with her. Look at the full moon. You can see the shape of the rabbit.

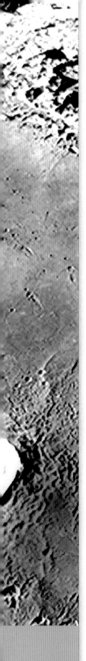

Gods and Chariots

This myth of the Inuit people in Greenland explains
why the moon and sun move in the sky. It also explains
why the shape of the moon seems to change.

The myth tells of Aningan. He was the god of the moon. Aningan chased his sister, Malina. She was the goddess of the sun. When Aningan chased Malina, he forgot to eat. Then he got thinner and thinner. He grew to his full size when he did eat again.

A Hindu myth explains why the moon moves across the sky. The myth says the god of the moon rides through the sky in a **chariot.** The chariot is pulled by white horses.

Soma, god of the moon, moves across the sky in a chariot.

Another Hindu myth explains why the moon seems to get smaller over time. The myth tells of a moon filled with a special potion. The gods drink the potion. As the gods drink, the moon becomes smaller.

potion: mix of drinks

Strategy Tool Kit
Make Connections
Are the myths about the moon similar to any other myths you have read or heard?

37

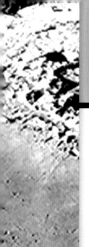

CHAPTER 2

Learning about the Moon

People liked to hear stories about the moon. They also tried to learn about the moon. Over time, people discovered facts about the moon.

The dark spots we see on the moon are craters that filled with lava. The lava hardened into smooth rock.

Up close, we can see the moon's craters.
We can also see that the moon has
valleys and mountains.

Before Telescopes

Greek scientists studied the moon about 2,000 years ago.
They did not have telescopes. They learned
about the moon by watching it.

The Greeks thought the dark, shadowy spots
on the moon were oceans. They also thought
the light parts were land. Plutarch was a Greek thinker.
He believed people lived on the moon.

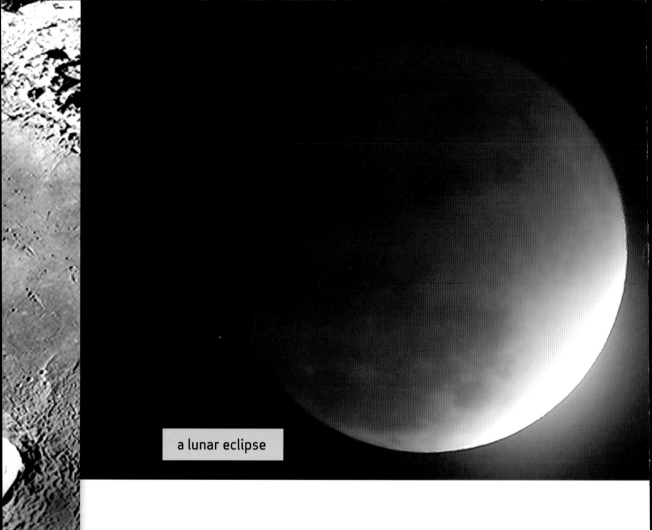

a lunar eclipse

One astronomer, Aristarchus, studied **lunar** eclipses. A lunar eclipse happens when the sun, Earth, and the moon are lined up perfectly with Earth in the middle. Earth creates a shadow. The shadow makes the moon appear darker than usual.

Lunar Eclipse

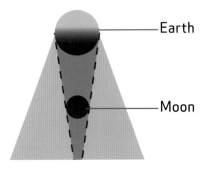

Sun

Earth

Moon

Earth blocks the sun's rays from reaching the moon.

Aristarchus watched the shadow. He was able to **calculate** how far away the moon and sun were from Earth. He also calculated their sizes.

Aristarchus figured out that the sun was much bigger than the moon. He also calculated that the sun was farther away. This made him believe that Earth revolved around the sun.

Strategy Tool Kit
Monitor Comprehension
Do you understand how a lunar eclipse occurs?

Galileo's first simple telescope made objects look large and close.

Galileo

In 1609 the study of the moon took a big leap forward. A scientist named Galileo built a telescope. He used it to view the moon closely. He discovered that the moon had mountains and valleys, like Earth.

Galileo's drawings from 1616 showed that the moon had landforms similar to Earth's.

Galileo made **sketches**, or drawings, of what he saw. People learned more about the moon from his sketches. He also helped improve the telescope. People were able to see even more of the night sky.

Stop and Think

How did early scientists study the moon? What did they learn and then pass on to later scientists?

43

Speaking of the Moon...

For years people have written about the moon.
These two **stanzas** are from a poem. The poem
was written in the 1870s.

Is the Moon Tired?

Is the moon tired? she looks so pale
Within her misty veil:
She scales the sky from east to west,
And takes no rest.

Before the coming of the night
The moon shows papery white;
Before the dawning of the day
She fades away.

from Sing-Song: A Nursery Rhyme Book
by Christina G. Rossetti (1830–1894)

scales: climbs

CHAPTER 3

Race to the Moon

Telescopes became more powerful as years went by. Space technology advanced. Scientists continued to learn more about the moon. By the 1950s the United States and the Soviet Union were in a "space race." Both countries wanted to explore space with satellites. They wanted to send people into space. They wanted to land people on the moon.

This photograph was taken by *Luna 3* in 1959. It shows the far side of the moon for the first time.

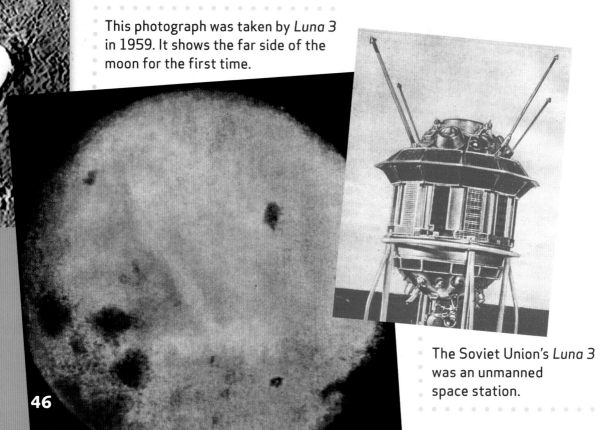

The Soviet Union's *Luna 3* was an unmanned space station.

Footprints can stay on the moon
for as long as one million years.
There is no wind to blow them away.

In 1969 the American spacecraft *Eagle* landed
on the moon. Two **astronauts** were the first people
to walk on the moon. Their names were Neil Armstrong
and Buzz Aldrin. Their footprints are still there!

The American moon landing was the start of a new era. The astronauts brought moon rocks back to Earth. They also brought moon soil back. They took close-up photographs of the surface of the moon.

era: time

This volcanic rock from the moon was brought back by the Apollo 15 lunar mission in 1971.

Scientists at NASA (the National Aeronautics and Space Administration) study data gathered from trips into space.

Scientists learned that the moon is very dry. The soil came from **volcanoes**. Scientists came up with ideas. They explained how and when the moon was formed. Scientists today believe that the moon is 4.6 billion years old.

Time Line of Moon Exploration

This time line shows some of the key advances that have helped us learn about the moon.

1609 Galileo looks at the moon through a telescope. He makes drawings of its landforms.

1840 Scientists take the first photos of the moon, using a telescope.

1957 The Soviet Union launches the first **artificial** satellite, *Sputnik I*, into space.

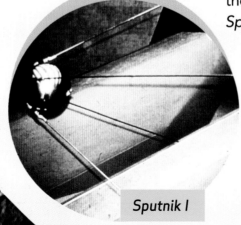

Sputnik I

Neil Armstrong on the moon

1966 The Soviet Union lands a spacecraft with no people on the moon.

1971 Two American astronauts spend more than three days on the moon.

1958 The United States launches its first satellite, the *Explorer*, into space.

1969 Two American astronauts walk on the moon.

Explorer

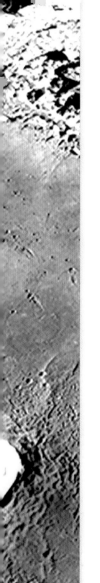

The moon looks like it rises each night because Earth is rotating.

People have always wanted to explain things they saw in the sky. Sometimes they made up stories to explain what they saw. Now science has helped us learn about the moon. Here are some facts we know.

🌙 The moon is shaped like an egg, not like a ball.

🌙 The moon revolves around Earth once every month.

🌙 There is no wind on the moon.

Strategy Tool Kit
Make Connections
Would you like to travel to the moon one day? Why or why not?

Over time people's ideas about the moon have changed. Many of the questions from the past are now answered. But there are still many things we don't know. There will be more answers to our questions about the moon as science advances.

Think Back
Selection 2

A Check Understanding ★

How did people of the past explain the moon in the night sky? How do their ideas differ from what we know now?

PRACTICE COMPANION **310**

B Understand Text Features ★★

An index is an alphabetical list of subjects found at the back of a book. Page numbers help you find the subjects within the book. Using the index, where would you find information about Galileo? Share your information with a partner.

C Share and Compare ★★

Make a list of past ideas about objects in space. Compare your list with a partner's list. Which ideas are the same? Which are different? Why?

D Think Critically ★★★★

Why do people study space? Use examples from the selection to explain.

Selection Connection

You have learned how people of the past were inspired by the night sky. In the next selection you will learn why people study space.

★★★★
Show What You Know

Think about the following: *telescopes*, *satellites*, and *space vehicles*. How do these things help us view space? Write your ideas.

Preview ▶   onl⦿ne coach

How do people view space today?
Preview pages 56–77. Then read *Twins* to find out.

Twins

by Dina McClellan
Illustrated by Steve Feldman

chapter 1 An Unexpected Offer

"Come on, girls, let's go for a drive!" said Mr. Williams, poking his head into the girls' room. Alex looked up and so did Andrea. They had been reading on their beds, and their father's offer had come as a surprise.

"But it's late!" said Alex.

"And it's a *school* night!" Andrea said.

"And it's freezing outside!"

"Just remember to put on warm clothes," said Mr. Williams. "This shouldn't take long! I'll meet you downstairs." And he was off.

The girls looked at each other and blinked.

"I don't get it," said Andrea.

"Me, neither," said Alex. "Unless . . ."

"Unless what?"

"Well, I was thinking," said Alex. "Our birthday is coming up next week. Maybe Dad's taking us to the mall to buy us a birthday present!"

Andrea's face lit up. "That must be it!"

The girls started jumping up and down on their beds.

"We'd better get ready," said Andrea, leaping to the floor, "before he changes his mind."

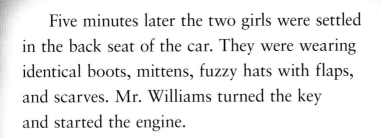

Five minutes later the two girls were settled in the back seat of the car. They were wearing identical boots, mittens, fuzzy hats with flaps, and scarves. Mr. Williams turned the key and started the engine.

"Seat belts, girls?"

Strategy Tool Kit
Ask and Answer Questions
What questions would you have for Mr. Williams?

"We're going to the Air and Space Museum.
Okay, girls?" said Mr. Williams. "It's been a while
since you've seen where I work."

"Sure, Dad!" they said together.

Alex shot her sister a look and whispered,
"That's not where the mall is!"

"He's just trying to <u>fool</u> us," Andrea whispered back.

"That must be it," said Alex. "Let's make him think we believe him."

"Right," said Andrea, "and then we'll act really surprised when we get to the mall!"

> fool: play a trick on

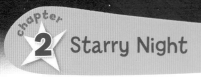

Soon they were driving along a <u>deserted</u> country road. To the girls' surprise, their father stopped the car and got out.

"Come and look!" he said. "There is something you will **marvel** at."

Alex and Andrea groaned. The girls dragged themselves out of the car and stood shivering next to their father. They had **blissful** thoughts about how warm the mall would be when they got there.

> deserted: empty

"It's **magnificent!**" cried Mr. Williams.

The girls turned their eyes toward the sky.
They'd never seen so many stars!
Alex tried to count them, but she kept
losing her place.

Strategy Tool Kit
Visualize
*How do you picture the sky
from the way the author
has described it?*

"How many stars can we see?" asked Andrea.

"Oh, about 3,000—without a telescope," answered Mr. Williams. "With a telescope, like the one we have at home, you could **observe** about 600,000 stars. But, if you used the one I have at the museum, you'd see millions of stars!"

"I know a star you can see during the day," said Alex. "The sun!"

"The sun isn't a star!" Andrea **protested**.

"Yes, it is," said Mr. Williams. "It's the closest star to Earth. But it's still pretty far away. If we went by car it would take us about 177 years to drive there!"

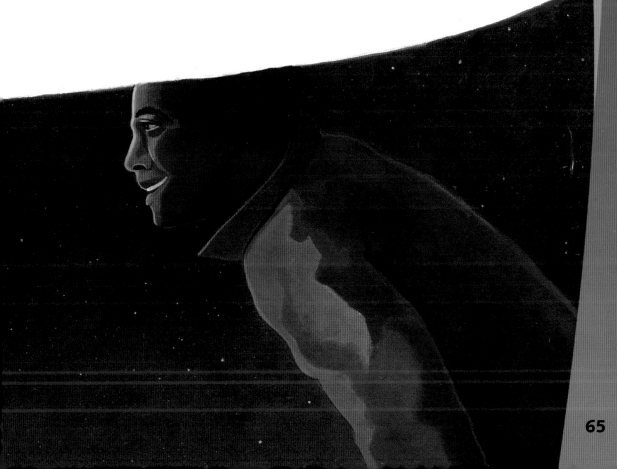

"The sun is so much bigger than the other stars!" said Andrea.

"That's because the other stars are so far away," said Mr. Williams. "Proxima Centauri, the next nearest star, is 25 trillion miles away! If you could reach the sun in one **gigantic** step, you'd need almost 300,000 of those gigantic steps to reach Proxima Centauri!"

"Can I see Proxima Centauri?" asked Alex.

"With a telescope you could,"
their father explained. "But you'd really be seeing
the light it gives off. And because light takes
time to travel, you'd be seeing the light it
gave off four years ago!"

"Like seeing into the past," said Andrea.

"I feel **miniature** when I think about how big everything is," Alex said.

"Me too," said her sister. "How about you, Dad?"

"Big and small at the same time," Mr. Williams said.

"Do stars really have points, Dad?" asked Alex.

"No—stars are huge round balls of hot, glowing gas. They just look pointy to us because we see them through moving layers of air and dust."

Stop and Think
What has the story told you about stars so far?

3 A Surprise

"Dad, do you know what next Tuesday is?" Andrea blurted out.

Alex poked her in the ribs.

Mr. Williams glanced at his wristwatch. "Next Tuesday it will be exactly 3,652 days since my wonderful twin girls were born."

The girls looked at each other and shrugged. There was no point trying to catch Dad. He never forgot their birthday.

> **shrugged:** lifted their shoulders

"So you girls want to know what kind of gift I'm getting you, right?"

"Right!"

"It's a surprise," he said.

"But, Dad!" cried the girls in **unison**.
"We thought we were going to the mall!"

"Why would you think that?" asked Mr. Williams.
"I told you we were going to the museum."

"Does this have something to do
with our birthday present?" Alex wanted to know.

"You could say that," said Mr. Williams
with a **sly** smile. "Actually, I'm keeping it in my office.
Now let's get back in the car. It's freezing."

"Give us a hint," Alex begged as the sisters piled into the backseat.

"No," said Mr. Williams. He started the car.

"Can we guess?" asked Andrea.

"You can try," Mr. Williams said.

Alex started off. "Is it one thing or two?"

"Two," said Mr. Williams. "But they're identical."

"Did you get us guitars?" asked Andrea, because she'd wanted to play.

"Did you get us laptops?" asked Alex, because their old one was broken.

Alex had an idea. "Does it have to do with *stars*?" she asked.

Mr. Williams tried to **disguise** a smile.

"You got us a *star*?"

"Of course not! I got you *two* stars. Twin stars for my twin girls."

"I was looking at a star **formation** and noticed two stars I hadn't seen before. It turns out I had discovered twin stars. I found them, so I get to name them. I thought I'd name them after *my* twin stars."

The girls beamed.

"There's a telescope in my office that will give you a clear view of my newly discovered stars, *Alexandra* and *Andrea*."

The girls hugged their father at the same time.

"Thanks, Dad!" the girls shouted.

"It's the best gift in the world!" said Andrea.

"Or *out* of this world!" said Alex, as they all laughed together.

> beamed: smiled joyfully

Strategy Tool Kit
Ask and Answer Questions
How do the twins feel about their birthday gift? Where can you find the answer in the text?

 **Think Back**
Selection 3

A Check Understanding ★

Think about the different tools used for space exploration. How do these tools help us get a better view of space today? PRACTICE COMPANION **339**

B Understand Literary Elements ★★

Imagery is language that describes how someone or something looks, sounds, feels, smells, or tastes. Look for examples of imagery in your selection. Share your examples with a partner.

C Share and Compare ★★

Make a list of space exploration tools discussed in your selection. Compare your list with a partner's list. Which tools are the same? Which tools are different? Why?

D Think Critically ★★★★

Why do people study space? Use examples from the selection to explain.

My Home Page

Think Ahead ▶
Selection 4

Focus Question: How might space be a part of our future?

Selection Connection

In *Twins* you learned how people view space today. In the next selection you will learn what inspires people to study space.

★★★★
Show What You Know

Think about the following: *space stations*; *minerals on other planets*; and *traveling to other planets*. How will these help space be a part of our future? Write your ideas. PRACTICE COMPANION 340

Preview ▶

How might space be a part of our future? Preview pages 80–102. Then read *To Neptune . . . and Back!* to find out.

TO NEPTUNE ...AND BACK!

by Kathy Zahler
Illustrated by Gary Swift

The Torres Journals

Pablo and Mariana Torres took off on a long trip on May 1, 2152. They traveled all the way to Neptune and back. Pablo and Mariana went to study the air and clouds around each of the planets they passed. They hoped to learn ways to cool Earth. People are concerned because the temperatures on Earth are **swelling**.

They kept this journal to tell about all they discovered on their trip.

MAY 1, 2152

Liftoff was great. We whipped around Earth.
Then we headed into space in a straight line.
We're traveling faster than anyone else ever has!

   Voyager 2 followed this same route
175 years ago. But spaceships are much faster today.
So we'll be back on Earth in just 12 years!
—*Mariana*

JANUARY 3, 2153

This trip requires two scientists. That's why my wife and I are together. Mariana studies weather and climate change. I study **chemistry**.

We passed Mars yesterday. Mariana wished we could stop on that planet. She wanted to feel a Martian dust storm. They can last for many months. The whole planet gets covered with dust.

But we're not landing anywhere. Our job is to learn what we can from a **distance** while zooming by in our spaceship.

I'm glad we didn't land. To me, that dust sounds nasty! —*Pablo*

MAY 20, 2153

Today's my birthday. It is a special treat to see Jupiter, the largest planet. Its **vast** size takes my breath away.

Pablo is viewing it through our telescope. I'm taking pictures of Jupiter's clouds.

Studying air and clouds is important. Earth's temperature keeps getting hotter. We need new ways to keep our planet cool. We may find some solutions by studying weather on other planets.

The mountains of Jupiter's largest moon are **remarkable**. They're shooting fire thousands of feet into the air.

Pablo says they're giant candles for my birthday! —*Mariana*

solutions: answers

Strategy Tool Kit
Ask and Answer Questions
What questions do you have about why Mariana and Pablo are making this trip?

APRIL 11, 2154

Mariana and I have now spent
more than two years in space. We play chess
a lot. She's much better than I am.
But sometimes I win. Ha!

We see Saturn. It's even more beautiful
than its pictures. Saturn's rings look solid.
But through the telescope, I see that they
are formed by millions of pieces of ice.

We never get too close to these "gas giants"
like Jupiter and Saturn. They are made mostly of gas.
If we get too close, the planet's gravity
will pull us down. So we send robots closer
to test Saturn's **atmosphere.** —*Pablo*

JUNE 15, 2155

Now we're in a long, dark gap between planets. We won't see another planet for more than a year.

We keep very busy. The robots have sent back **samples** from the three planets. In our lab we run all kinds of tests on the planets' air.

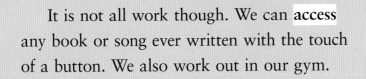

It is not all work though. We can **access** any book or song ever written with the touch of a button. We also work out in our gym.

We play chess often. Sometimes I let Pablo win. He gets so excited when he does! —*Mariana*

Stop and Think
What have you learned about each of the planets that Mariana and Pablo have seen so far?

89

MARCH 27, 2156

We have learned a lot so far. And we have sent reports back to Earth.

We still have the ice giants to see. Uranus and Neptune are far from the sun. They are very cold.

Meanwhile, we stay in touch with friends and family at home. We talk to them on a big computer screen. They joke with us and give us news. I told my brother how many times I beat Mariana at chess. He was surprised! —*Pablo*

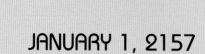

JANUARY 1, 2157

Happy New Year, Earth!

We are nearing Uranus. We
call it a fuzzy blue tennis ball.
Its atmosphere is made of heavy elements.
We see the sun's light **reflect** off the heavy gas.
That makes Uranus <u>appear</u>
fuzzy and blue-green.

appear: look

Neptune is about a billion miles farther from Uranus. But I can't wait to study it! Big clouds of gas surround Neptune. Pablo and I will study them. —*Mariana*

Strategy Tool Kit
Make Connections
Have you ever traveled to learn about something? Were you excited along the way?

MAY 20, 2157

It's Mariana's birthday again. I baked a cake in our tiny kitchen. And I wrote her name in icing. I said I made the cake just for her. She laughed and said, "We are alone in the spaceship. Who else would you make it for?"

The news from Earth is worrisome. They are having bad storms. Crops are being ruined. Soon it may be hard to grow anything.

We hope our work will help Earth. Mariana keeps wondering about Neptune's clouds. But we won't see Neptune until next year. —*Pablo*

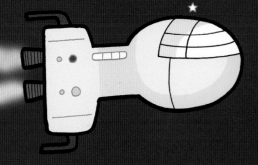

JUNE 10, 2158

We made it! We have traveled farther
than anyone else ever has. We can see Neptune
right now.

   The winds blow at 700 miles per hour down there.
Storms on Neptune look like huge, dark spots.
Some of them can be as large as Earth.
We are examining these storms through our telescope.

I can finally see Neptune's clouds! They are blue and very cold. They are much bigger than any clouds on Earth. They make Neptune look like it has stripes. —*Mariana*

SEPTEMBER 20, 2158

We have been in space for more than six years. Right now, we're both working hard. We study hundreds of samples each day. Then we put them in special boxes. Our robots take them back to Earth.

Neptune has rings like Saturn's. No one is sure about what those rings are made of. I plan to find out!

Mariana wants to learn how Neptune's clouds are made. She also wants to know how Neptune's temperature affects them. The center of Neptune puts out much more heat than the center of Uranus. Nobody knows why. Mariana thinks studying Neptune's atmosphere may help us fix Earth's climate! —*Pablo*

Strategy Tool Kit
Ask and Answer Questions
Why does studying Neptune's clouds seem like a good way to learn about Earth's climate? Where could you find the answers?

DECEMBER 31, 2158

Is it another new year already? Time flies.

Speaking of flying, we did some tricky flying today. We had to build up speed as we circled Neptune. Then we used our speed to whip us quickly back toward Uranus.

We have studied Neptune for six months. We have lots of encouraging data to look over and think about on our trip home.

What we learned on Neptune just may help scientists fix our planet. On Earth people are already calling us heroes. —*Mariana*

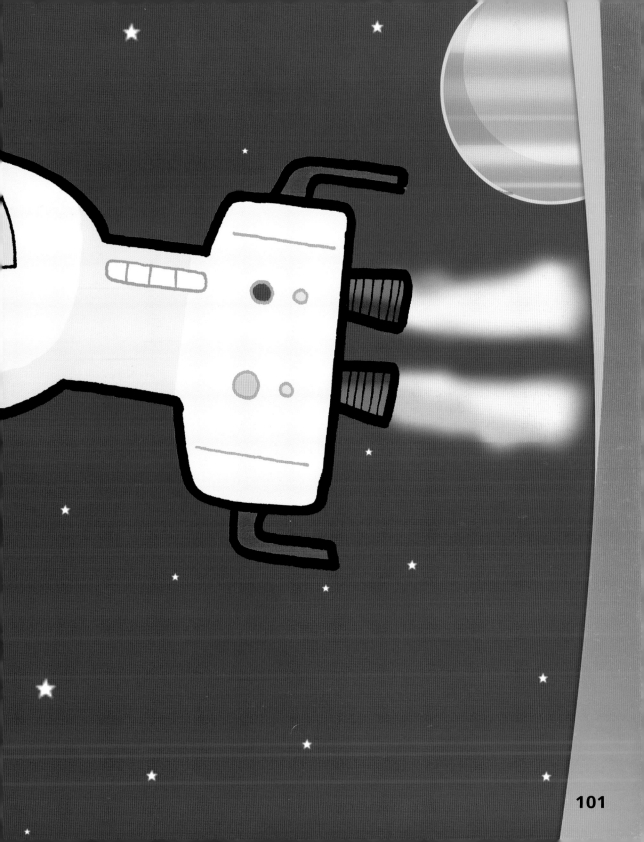

MAY 20, 2163

This is probably Mariana's last birthday in space. We'll be home in about eight months. As a gift, I made her a chess set. All the planets we studied appear on the board.

I'm sure we'll play a game tonight. I hope I win!
—*Pablo*

Focus Question: How might space be a part of our future?

A ## Check Understanding ★

Using ideas from the selection, make a list of the ways space may be a part of our future. Do you think these events will happen? | PRACTICE COMPANION **359**

B ## Understand Literary Elements ★★

A motive is the reason why a character does something. Motives tell you what a character wants. What are Mariana's and Pablo's motives for going to Neptune? What do these tell you about the characters? Discuss your answers with a partner.

C ## Share and Compare ★★

With a partner, compare your list of the ways space may be a part of our future. How does your partner's list differ from yours? How is it the same?

D ## Think Critically ★★★★

Why do people study space? Use examples from the selection to explain.

My Home Page

Why do people study space?

Use these activities to show what you've learned about the theme question.

Design and Create

1. Imagine that you discovered a new constellation. Design your own model of it.

2. Draw your constellation on black construction paper. Cut out small holes for stars to form the shape of the constellation.

3. Shine a light behind the paper to see the shape that the stars would make in the sky.

Multimedia

1. With a partner, design two Web pages about space and space exploration. Include the text and pictures that you want on your Web pages.

2. Present your Web page designs to the class.

Book Club

1. Choose your favorite selection from the unit. Tell your group why you chose it.

2. Read your favorite part aloud.

3. Search for other books about space to read and share.

Be an Author

1. Imagine that your town is located on the moon.

2. Write a story that describes your daily life. Think about how life on the moon is different from the life you live on Earth. Be sure to include dialogue between characters.

3. Read your story to a friend.

Glossary

access (ak′ ses) *v.* to get at;
We can access the basement by using the stairs near the kitchen. **89**

artificial (är′ tə fish′ əl) *adj.* made by humans rather than by nature;
The artificial lake was made by pumping in water from underground pipes. **50**

astronaut (as′ trə nôt′) *n.* a person who travels in space;
One astronaut controlled the spaceship, and the other astronaut took a spacewalk. **47**

astronomer (ə stron′ ə mər) *n.* a person who studies the moon, stars, planets, and other heavenly bodies;
An astronomer spoke to our class about the Milky Way. **6**

atmosphere (at′ mə sfîr′) *n.* the layer of gases that surrounds a planet;
Earth's atmosphere protects us. **86**

awe (ô) *n.* wonder, fear, or respect;
We looked at the statue of Abraham Lincoln with great awe. **10**

blissful (blis′ fəl) *adj.* extremely happy;
My blissful parents could not stop smiling at my baby brother. **62**

calculate (kal′ kyə lāt′) *v.* to estimate or figure out mathematically;
I will calculate how much time I spent building this birdhouse. **41**

chariot (char′ ē ət) *n.* a two-wheeled, horse-drawn vehicle used in ancient times;
Four white horses pulled the chariot into battle. **36**

chemistry (kem′ i strē) *n.* the science that deals with substances, what they are made of, and what their features are;
My sister studies chemistry and does some interesting experiments. **82**

comet (kom′ it) *n.* a bright object in space that has a long tail of light when it gets close to the sun;
A comet can sometimes be seen streaking across the night sky. **26**

disguise (dis gīz′) *v.* to change appearance in order to hide oneself;
Yael tried to disguise himself with a mask. **76**

distance (dis′ təns) *n.* the space between two points;
What is the distance between the two goals on a soccer field? **82**

dome (dōm) *n.* a rounded roof or ceiling;
The dome on the stadium could be seen from miles away. **18**

eager (ē′ gər) *adj.* wanting to do something very much;
We were eager to go to the movie on opening day. **12**

examine (ig zam′ in) *v.* to look at and check closely;
The doctor will examine my ears with a small light. **96**

formation (fôr mā′ shən) *n.* something that is made, arranged, or formed, as in a pattern;
We arranged the paper clips in a formation that looked like a house. **77**

gigantic (jī gan′ tik) *adj.* huge, like a giant;
A gigantic thundercloud darkened the whole sky. **66**

gravity (gra′ vi tē) *n.* the force that pulls things toward Earth;
Gravity is what makes a plate hit the floor when it falls off a table. **23**

immortal (i môr′ tl) *adj.* living forever;
The old video of my great-grandparents made them seem immortal. **33**

improve (im pro̅o̅v′) *v.* to make something better;
Computer manufacturers try to improve their products each time they build a new model. **12**

intrigue (in trēg′) *v.* to make curious or interested;
Crinkly paper will often intrigue a little kitten. **9**

lunar (lo̅o̅′ nər) *adj.* having to do with the moon;
When the moon was full, we could see the dark and light spots on the lunar surface. **40**

magnificent (mag ni′ fə sənt) *adj.* very grand and beautiful;
The queen wore a magnificent crown with many beautiful gems. **63**

marvel (mär′ vəl) *v.* to feel a sense of wonder or astonishment;
You will marvel when you see the acrobats do their routine. **62**

miniature (min′ ē ə cho̅o̅r′) *adj.* something very small for its kind;
Mrs. Meade's miniature poodle fits in her backpack. **68**

myth (mith) *n.* a story that tries to explain a natural event or a belief;
Last week we read a Greek myth about a young man who tried to touch the sun. **32**

observe (əb zûrv′) *v.* to see with careful attention;
The class will observe how the plant grows. **64**

protest (prə test′) *v.* to object to something;
I heard Bobby protest loudly when the coach benched him during practice. **65**

reflect (ri flekt′) *v.* to give back, bounce off;
A car's side mirrors reflect images of what is behind it. **92**

remarkable (ri mär′ kə bəl) *adj.* worthy of being noticed; unusual;
The giant dinosaur skeleton in the museum is remarkable. **85**

revolve (ri volv′) *v.* to move in a circle around a center point;
The little children revolve in a circle around their teacher as they sing. **7**

rotate (rō′ tāt) *v.* to turn on an axis;
The chickens rotate in the big ovens behind the deli counter at the store. **7**

sample (sam′ pəl) *n.* a small part of something that shows what the whole is like;
I tasted a sample of the bread. **88**

section (sek′ shən) *n.* a part of a whole; a piece;
Grandma cut the apple into pieces and gave each of us a section. **16**

sketch (skech) *n.* a rough drawing;
Agnes will make a sketch of the wooden toy. **43**

sly (slī) *adj.* clever; up to a little bit of mischief;
Marietta had a sly look on her face as she was planning the party. **73**

sophisticated (sə fis′ ti kā′ tid) *adj.* having knowledge and experience in the ways of the world;
The sophisticated traveler told us about her visit to France. **14**

stanza (stan′ zə) *n.* a group of lines in a poem;
The last stanza of that poem has some beautiful rhymes. **44**

swell (swel) *adj.* to increase;
When the candy fell to the ground, the number of ants began to swell. **80**

telescope (te′ lə skōp′) *n.* an instrument that makes faraway objects seem larger and closer;
We use the telescope to get a closer look at the moon's surface. **10**

unison (yōō′ ni sən) *n.* movements or sounds done at the same time;
The line of dancers kicked their legs in perfect unison. **72**

vast (vast) *adj.* very great in size;
Lake Michigan looks as vast as an ocean, but it is not. **84**

volcano (vol kā′ nō) *n.* an opening in Earth's crust through which hot lava and molten rock come out;
Much of the island's rich soil comes from the cooled lava that came out of the volcano. **49**

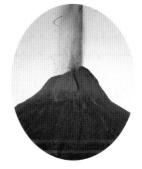

Index

Acknowledgments

Photo Credits: Cover ©Pete Oxford/Minden Pictures; **4** ©NASA; **5** (tl) ©Alamy Images, (tr) ©Leda_d/Shutterstock, (bl) ©Comstock Images/Alamy, (br) ©NASA; **6** ©Photo Courtesy of NASA/Corbis; **6–27** (bkgd, thru-out) ©Photolink/Getty Images; **7** ©National Oceanic and Atmospheric Administration; **8** ©Alamy Images; **9** ©Bettmann/Corbis; **10–11** ©Brand X Pictures/Punchstock; **11** ©Bettmann/Corbis; **12** (l) ©Photodisc/Getty Images, (r) ©Stockbyte/Getty Images; **13** ©Tony Hallas/Science Faction/Corbis; **15** ©Roger Ressmeyer/Corbis; **16–17** ©Royal Astronomical Society/Photo Researchers, Inc.; **18** ©Don Smetzer/Alamy; **19** ©Lowell Observatory/AP Images; **20** ©NASA; **21** ©Patrick Phair; **23** ©Antonio M. Rosario/Getty Images; **24** ©Friedrich Saurer/Alamy; **26** ©Peter Arnold, Inc./Alamy; **27** ©Will Yurman/AP Images; **28** ©Photo Courtesy of NASA/Corbis; **29** (l) ©Leda_d/Shutterstock, (r) ©Alamy Images; **30** ©Digital Stock/Corbis; **30–52** (bkgd) ©NASA; **31** (l) ©Taesam Do/Botanica/GettyImages, (r) ©Gallo Images-Shem Compion/Getty Images; **32, 33** ©NASA; **38** ©Digital Stock/Corbis; **39** ©NASA; **40–41** ©Marc Crumpler/Getty Images; **41** ©McGraw-Hill Companies Inc.; **42** ©The Granger Collection, New York; **43** ©The Granger Collection, New York; **46** ©NASA; **47** ©NASA Center; **48** ©Roger Ressmeyer/Corbis; **49** ©Roger Ressmeyer/Corbis; **50** ©NASA; **50–51** ©NASA; **51** ©NASA; **53** ©Renaud Visage/Getty Images; **54** ©Taylor S. Kennedy/Getty Images; **55** (t) ©NASA, (b) ©Comstock Images/Alamy; **79** (t) ©Brand X Pictures/PunchStock, (b) ©Pixtal/Agefotostock.

Art Credits: 32, 33 ©The McGraw-Hill Companies, Inc./Robert Schuster; **34–35, 36–37, 44–45** ©The McGraw-Hill Companies, Inc./Pamela Becker; **52** ©McGraw-Hill Companies, Inc./Argosy; **56–78** ©The McGraw-Hill Companies, Inc./Steve Feldman; **80–103** ©The McGraw-Hill Companies, Inc./Gary Swift.